For my brothers

NEW YORK

Photography by Mark Crosby

Foreword by Charlie Smith

UNIVERSE

First published in the United States of
America in 2000 by
UNIVERSE PUBLISHING
A Division of Rizzoli International
Publications, Inc.
300 Park Avenue South
New York, NY 10010

2000 2001 2002 2003 2004 2005 / 10 9 8
7 6 5 4 3 2 1

Printed in Italy

Library of Congress Catalog Card Number:
00-133701

RIGHT: A certain midtown landmark makes an imperious impression on its fashion district neighbors.

Foreword

BY CHARLIE SMITH

In this world that has no beginning or end the light is sometimes autumnal for years. In the parks, the light draws fanciful colors out of the heaped-up bushes. Sometimes the light is brisk, honed, an eidolic impersonal unsurveyed light that falls like diamond and glass chips on the heads of girls walking to school. Sometimes it is murky, vague, an unfinished light, hurried into place. Sometimes it seems about to answer the most important question possible. Love comes and goes and comes again in such a light. Sometimes, down some streets, in such a light, you think you can see all the way to the Far West, but it is only Hoboken. The buildings (in New York City) hold back not only light but the dark, a dark that collects in the stones and is comforted there.

In such a city, a city that makes itself up as it goes along—that believes it does—makes itself out of happenstance and hard work, out of singing and drudgery and love and grievances, out of fabricators and screechers and bit players and artists learning to love whatever is in front of their eyes, in such a city small moments of consummation, of affinity, in the stillness of the heart's longing satisfied, take on an immense importance. They take on a vast and conscious meaning, someone says. All this is alluded to in Mark Crosby's extraordinary photographs. They point out that sometimes blue hair is the same blue as a blue umbrella. Here it is snowing on yellow wands of forsythia—yellow wands of sunshine—somewhere out in the park.

The quiet moment, the one almost mentioned, earned or come on by chance, begins as you step from the limo you've taken back from some caper in Spanish Harlem or Morningside Heights. There now in SoHo on the corner of Spring and Lafayette someone moves past you out of the million snowy footprints. Maybe it's the bicycle parked in the snow, or maybe it's the long street opening casually before you, or the trim light in the gray sky that is the same sky that rises at dawn out of the Lower Bay, or maybe it's only the passersby in their dark and annealing outfits, or maybe it's the colors—the yellow and the blue—still going strong on the storefronts, or maybe it's only the mix of everything, but your heart surges with love for the city, which is the same love at this moment as the love of being alive. You go quiet inside. And the quiet that is in you becomes the quiet outside you—the city not stalled, not even slowed down, but for once its pace meets your own—and you experience in your bones the strong thrust of life moving through all things.

These photographs glide and hover, they swoop and rustle, they descend through atmospheres of bravado and fashion into the long insistence of a look, into areaways, across parks and down streets that are so beautiful you want to spend whatever time you must searching them out. You want to move your permanent residence to one of these streets. Maybe 10th or Water Street or 106th. Someone has put flowers into an urn in one of the park's open places. A child in a suit made of leaves watches a parade pass. One color, say blue, heretofore unpublished in this life, replaces another. The city is its own acrobat, its archivist, opiner, surehand, alienist, conniver, its long-range thinker, its little girl with a face like a prayer. It comes and goes at will and says what it thinks and never apologizes, and never stops apologizing. Over there a boy in red turns a handstand. The shadows of the tallest buildings fall across the backs of apartment houses, bringing relief from the summer heat and setting free another life, a life that needs shade to thrive. There is never enough time for everything, but then everything gets done. We are always celebrating something. Someone is always asking if you heard that, if you saw that. Yes, yes, of course you heard it, of course you saw it. Or you will soon. Or you'll simply say you did.

Someone has planted spruce trees in a window box. At Jefferson Market it is 4:30 in the afternoon on fall's first day. Someone looks out a window at a glossy patch of green grass, at a troop in white hats passing, at an abutment as stern as a gravestone, at an architectural elevation leading the eye across and up into the sky that is all the wilderness one needs. The city leans into itself, explaining as it goes. Gold portals and marquees report the answers to profound

philosophical questions. Day becomes night without telling anyone. Children walk home under a cumulus of red and white balloons. Wherever you are you can get somewhere else, maybe not at this moment, but soon. There is always somewhere else to go. On the Lower East Side, outside a storefront above which business suits hang like the trophies of kings, two men shake hands. They could be brothers, they could be friends, they could be members of some secret organization. The suits are turned to the light like sunflowers. The lamp pole is covered with the remnants of flyers bespeaking hope for the many, surcease of pain and an answer to trouble. Some woman, someone no one knows, casts a noncommittal eye at the merchandise. Life will go on from here. The next moment will begin here.

The city's wild to hook up with whatever will have it—with whomever—but then it changes its mind. Today some sweetness and then a fistfight. The city is so grand it's not sure it's real. For a second, everyone believes what he says. This passes. And the days roll over themselves—sometimes begging pardon—and the mysterious bridges, frail and enduring, sibilant as a song on love's first night, unscroll, heading away to some place we have never been and never wanted to go. How long, one thinks, before I find the one who loves me? How long before I can show what is inside me? The city explains nothing. Promises nothing. Offers nothing but what the dark offers, the dark, that is, broken open by light.

What started in the off precincts, and on streets barely sentient, in rushed breathing and hope as thin as a cracker, has unfolded into high-soarings and variables, into a tough and sentimental consciousness that refuses to be brokered or repealed. A vast carelessness finds its way to refinements. Vulgarity learns to dance. Lives crackle, catch fire and shed light. Two boys—it's too late now even to ask who they are—walk home down a parade avenue. The names of life are painted on the backs of passersby, on building fronts and on the air around them. The sky, what's left of it today, is blue to the core, bluer than any sky before or since. A pink and white arch has drifted in from somewhere and hangs like the gate of heaven over the street. There is still so much to talk about. There is still so much to see. How good it is to find you, if only for a moment.

Preface

BY MARK CROSBY

When Rizzoli's Universe Publishing asked me to photograph New York for a year and turn in an edit of my best shots for a book, I accepted the opportunity without hesitation, because I knew it would be a wonderful chance to share with so many others what I find so enthralling about this city. Naturally any self-respecting photography book on New York would cry out for its fair share of landmarks and skylines, and, to be sure, Universe and I compared notes early on about which ones the book should include. What would appear in the rest of the book was entirely up to me, however, and it was this material that interested me the most. I say this because, while I enjoyed immensely the chance to photograph New York's landmarks, I far more enjoyed finding those serendipitous images that convey what it is like to actually dwell within and among the familiar icons of the world's most famous cityscape. So

you will find that this book is filled with people. They're packed into concert halls and opera houses, browsing in museums and galleries, eating at restaurants and cafes, participating in parades or marathons, or simply crossing the street—each photograph an evanescent gesture or expression portraying the city's surpassing ability to captivate and inspire anyone fortunate enough to spend time here.

On the other hand, being on foot amidst New York's miraculous architecture presented me with continually realigning juxtapositions of spires, facades, bridges, and statuary. And when these architectural elements are compounded by the changing play of ambient light, street light, and weather they, too, have their fleeting and never again moments.

It has been a rare gift to be able to share with you through this book the best moments from a year of taking photographs (nearly 10,000) of New York and New Yorkers, and I am indebted to Universe and its publisher, Charles Miers, for the opportunity. During that year, many friends gave generously of their time and talents toward the making of this book, and I wish to thank them by name. Dayton Haigney, Pete Doyle, Fred Varone, Peter Clark, David Kitto, and Elisabeth Pearson helped me gain access to private spaces, as well as places high above. Hampton Sides, Kristen Renney, Shannon Wandell, David Leitch, Kathy Grafton, and particularly my sisters-in-law Elizabeth Crosby and Molly Crosby helped me with the text and quotations appearing in this book. Kevin McKiernan helped me secure permissions necessary to use some of the quotations. Tom Hubbard, Dan Gentile, and the staff of Time Life Photo Center developed my film with courtesy, timeliness, and professionalism.

In addition to the contributions and friendship of those above, I am grateful for the sustaining encouragement and interest of my family and of my friends Chris Browder, Daniel Fetterman, Bruce Mandelbaum, Stan Brent, Jordan Kessler, Richard Hershenson, David Russell, Charlie Smith, Katie Keck, Julie Wenzell, Mark Chalfant, Maggie Hopp, Steve Burns, Lisa Glenn, Paul Skurman, Bob Strickland, Hope Harris, Mark and Lisa Lencke, Chip Brookhart, Breck Bolton, Todd Davidson, Lee Findlay, Brian Jones, Kevin Cole, Marylou Awiakta, and Hugh Martin.

Finally, I wish to extend a special thanks to Susan Gudeon, who provided me with invaluable administrative and editorial assistance throughout the development of the book; to my (now gainfully employed) friend Jim Crutchfield, who stood nearby while many of these shots were taken, helping me carry equipment or making me look like I was entitled to cross a police barricade once in a while; and to my editors at Universe, Abigail Wilentz and Julia Gaviria, and particularly, the designer of the book, Amelia Costigan, each of whom honored my highest efforts with their own.

RIGHT: Hell's Gate, a swift-current tributary connecting the East River and Long Island Sound, reflects the remains of the day.

PREVIOUS PAGE: Since the mid 1960s the upper stories of the Empire State Building have been floodlit in an array of colors marking different events and occasions. Here, a sapphire suit is donned to celebrate the birthday of old Blue Eyes himself, Frank Sinatra.

FOLLOWING PAGES: Dealing a tough blow to a thriving ferry business that, by 1870, carried over 100,000 passengers a day between Brooklyn and downtown Manhattan, the Brooklyn Bridge opened to world acclaim in 1883. Ironically, its creator was killed in a ferry accident in 1869, two years into the construction of the bridge.

Over the great bridge, with the sunlight through the girders making a constant flicker upon the moving cars, with the city rising up across the river in white heaps and sugar lumps all built with a wish out of non-olfactory money. The city seen from the Queensboro Bridge is always the city seen for the first time, in its first wild promise of all the mystery and the beauty in the world. . . ."Anything can happen now that we've slid over this bridge," I thought; "anything at all. . . ."

— F. Scott Fitzgerald, *The Great Gatsby*

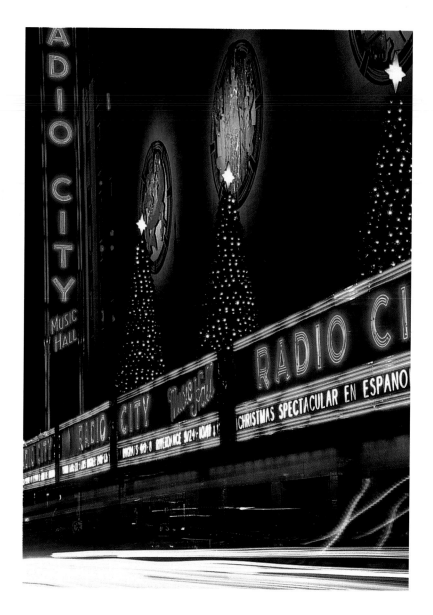

ABOVE: Opened in 1932 and restored to its original splendor in 1999, Radio City Music Hall remains as popular as ever and continues to host star entertainment, including its Christmas Spectacular featuring the Radio City Rockettes.

RIGHT: The Promenade provides a wonderful introduction to Rockefeller Center, momentarily in red for a tourism promotion.

We shape our buildings;

thereafter they shape us.

—Winston Churchill

Sole occupants of a swatch of rarified air above Midtown, these famous neighbors have kept an unobstructed eye on each other for nearly three-quarters of a century.

Ah, what can ever be more stately and admirable to me than mast-hemm'd Manhattan? / River and sunset and scallop-edg'd waves of flood-tide? / The sea-gulls oscillating their bodies, the hay-boat in the twilight, and the belated lighter?

Flow on, river! flow with the flood-tide, and ebb with the ebb-tide! Frolic on, crested and scallop-edg'd waves! / Gorgeous clouds of the sunset! drench with your splendor me, or the men / and women generations after me!

Cross from shore to shore, countless crowds of passengers! / Stand up, tall masts of Mannahatta! stand up, beautiful hills of Brooklyn! Throb, baffled and curious brain! throw out questions and answers! / Suspend here and everywhere, eternal float of solution!

— **Walt Whitman,** *"Crossing Brooklyn Ferry"*

LEFT: The United Nations Secretariat Building rises majestically above the graceful curving lines of its adjoining General Assembly Hall.

ABOVE: Although located in Manhattan between First Avenue and the East River, the UN is not considered part of the city, nor even the United States, and has its own police force, post office, and fire department.

Everywhere in the world, music enhances a hall, with
one exception: Carnegie Hall enhances the music.

—Isaac Stern

How do you get there? Practice, practice, practice. Since its opening in
1891, 2800-seat Carnegie Hall, long praised for its acoustic excellence,
has hosted over 50,000 musical and non-musical events.

ABOVE: Jockeys welcome diners to The 21 Club, named for its address at 21 West 52nd Street. Originally a speakeasy, its wine cellar still has a secret entrance (but don't tell anyone).

RIGHT: Cartier acquired its Renaissance mansion flagship store in 1917 in exchange for a pearl necklace.

The U.S. Marines Corps display their well-honed precision and march up Fifth Avenue in the annual St. Patrick's Day Parade.

RIGHT: Limestone residential terraces face south from the exclusive precinct of Manhattan's Upper East Side.

PREVIOUS SPREAD: Each March, Fifth Avenue is overtaken by the St. Patrick's Day Parade, whose countless, richly attired bands of bagpipes summon all within earshot. The parade was first held in 1766 and came under the auspices of its present organizer, the Ancient Order of the Hibernians, in the 1850s.

FOLLOWING PAGE LEFT: Students rehearse at the Joffrey Ballet School on Sixth Avenue in Greenwich Village.

FOLLOWING PAGE RIGHT: A young art student sketches Greco-Roman busts grouped for display at the Metropolitan Museum of Art.

I grew familiar with the palatial townhouses and high-rise penthouses on the Upper East Side with marble staircases, wide and steep and long, and Steinway grands which Gershwin had played on right in these rooms. . . . One could in these moments stand on the outside balconies and absorb the music from the distance and tinkle the ice in your glass and watch the great lights of Manhattan come on.

— **Willie Morris,** *New York Days*

LEFT: Among the Met's most popular permanent exhibits are its many suits of armor, axes, maces, swords, and, finally, pistols, "whose offensive strength," as one guidebook puts it, "brought to a close the armorer's trade."

ABOVE: Flanking wings were added in the 1920s to the Fifth Avenue facade of the Metropolitan Museum of Art. The Met was founded in 1870.

ABOVE: The ancient Temple of Dendur is the centerpiece of the Met's Egyptian art collection, second in size only to the one in Cairo.

RIGHT: The Met's art collection is the largest in the Western Hemisphere, with over two million objects, one larger example of which appears to have escaped notice of this intent visitor.

FOLLOWING PAGES: The Guggenheim Museum, with its widening spiral of hand-plastered concrete, opened on Fifth Avenue in 1959. Wright's intent for the spiral was to allow a continuous viewing of paintings while walking the spiral "from top to bottom."

ABOVE: The Guggenheim's famous spiral more closely resembles the jutting bow of a luxury liner when seen in this reflection.

LEFT: A Times Square souvenir shop traffics in a little local color.

The Empire State Building, as seen from the promenade of New Jersey's Liberty State Park.

No **good opera plot** *can be sensible,*

for people do not sing when they

are feeling sensible.

— W. H. Auden

A sold-out house is on hand for the Metropolitan Opera's performance of *La Traviata*. The opera company was founded in 1883 and moved to its present Lincoln Center home in 1966.

The New York Philharmonic and its esteemed conductor, the maestro Kurt Masur, gracefully accept accolades from an appreciative audience following a "Live from Lincoln Center Performance" simultaneously broadcast by radio across the nation.

Lincoln Center, home to ten performing arts companies, including the New York Philharmonic, the New York City Ballet, and the Metropolitan Opera, is the largest performing arts complex in the United States, attracting to its events nearly 500,000 visitors a year.

Crossing the Street in New York

keeps old people young—if they make it.

— Andy Rooney

THE CITY OF NEW YORK

HORSE DRAWN CAB

1071

DEPT OF CONSUMER AFFAIRS

LEFT: On fair weather days, a hansom cab may still be hailed on Central Park South, albeit for a handsome fare.

ABOVE: Anchoring Manhattan's historic Upper West Side is the venerable American Museum of Natural History.

—◆—

We ate lunch at the cafeteria in the park. Afterwards, avoiding the zoo (Holly said she couldn't bear to see anything in a cage), we giggled, ran, sang along the paths toward the old wooden boathouse, now gone. Leaves floated on the lake; on the shore, a park-man was fanning a bonfire of them, and the smoke, rising like Indian signals, was the only smudge on the quivering air. Aprils have never meant much to me, autumns seem that season of beginning, spring; which is how I felt sitting with Holly on the railings of the boathouse porch.

— **Truman Capote,** *Breakfast at Tiffany's*

—◆—

The Boathouse in Central Park provides the perfect Indian summer diversion, whether enjoying a meal or working it off.

FOLLOWING PAGE LEFT: The twin sunlit spires of the El Dorado apartment building are visible from across Central Park's Sheep's Meadow.

FOLLOWING PAGE RIGHT: The chain-link perimeter of the Central Park Reservoir is traced by a 1.5-mile running track favored by long-distance enthusiasts. Marathon anyone?

ABOVE: A talented band of bronze animals takes to a revolving stage each hour on the hour at this Central Park clock, near the Children's Zoo.

BELOW: Alice, in a winter wonderland, will be covered with climbing children, come spring.

LEFT: Bethesda Terrace, Central Park's formal focal point, awaits warmer weather.

RIGHT: Belvedere Castle located near the Great Lawn in the center of Central Park remains in use as a weather station for the city. In earlier times, a hoisted white banner with a red ball in the center signaled that the park's various ponds were safe for skating.

The graceful arch of a Central Park's Bow Bridge is made more so by winter's touch.

A masterpiece of balconies and beaux-arts brilliance, the Ansonia apartment building, on the Upper West Side, has listed among its residents Babe Ruth, Enrico Caruso, and Igor Stravinsky.

FOLLOWING PAGE LEFT: Using singular state of the art technology, the American Museum of Natural History's new planetarium goes far to explain a concept little understood by most New Yorkers: space.

FOLLOWING PAGE RIGHT: The American Museum of Natural History, taking up four city blocks between 77th and 81st Street on the Upper West Side, houses over 32 million specimens and artifacts and sponsors 100 research expeditions every year to all parts of the world.

t was as if the West End had been raked over by a gigantic harrow and planted with seeds of steel and stone; now as the century turned, the avenues had begun to erupt in strange, immense growths: modern flowers with veins of steel, bursting out of bedrock. . . .

— **Steven Millhauser,** *Martin Dressler*

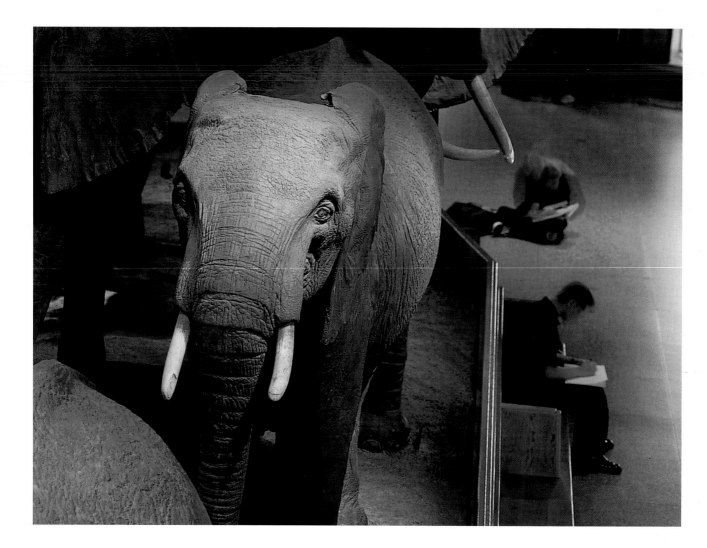

ABOVE: To make a lifelike rendition of this elephant group, part of the American Museum of Natural History's Hall of African Mammals, the museum's taxidermists (working in the 1930s) first mounted the elephant bones in the desired pose; then laid on in clay each muscle and tendon. Next the skins were fitted over the sculptures and molded to the musculature, and glass eyes were added.

RIGHT: These dinosaur bones in the Roosevelt Rotunda of the American Museum of Natural History are casts from the real thing (also in the museum), which dates back about 140–150 million years.

ABOVE: An early arrival of the recent spate of bistros taking Manhattan by storm, Balthazar, at Crosby and Spring Streets in SoHo, remains ever popular, except with those who expect a table without a reservation.

PREVIOUS PAGES: Over thirty thousand epicures a week flock to Zabar's on Broadway at 80th Street for its vast array of cheeses (over four hundred kinds), cured meats, and smoked fish.

This Manhattan resident and its owner appear well suited for each other.

———◆———

Commuters give the city its tidal restlessness; natives give it solidity and continuity; but the settlers give it passion. And whether it is a farmer arriving from Italy to set up a small grocery store in a slum, or a young girl arriving from a small town in Mississippi to escape the indignity of being observed by her neighbors, or a boy arriving from the Corn Belt with a manuscript in his suitcase and a pain in his heart, it makes no difference: each embraces New York with the intense excitement of first love, each absorbs New York with the fresh eyes of an adventurer, each generates heat and light to dwarf the Consolidated Edison Company.

— **E. B. White,** *Here is New York*

———◆———

Time and train wait for no man at Grand Central Terminal. Since its celebrated opening in 1913, countless commuters from upstate and beyond start and end their work day by passing through here.

If ever there was an aviary overstocked with jays
it is that Yaptown-on-the-Hudson, called New York.

— O. Henry, The Gentle Grafter,
"A Tempered Wind"

RIGHT: Times Square, as seen from 42nd Street, between Broadway and Eighth Avenue.

PREVIOUS PAGES: The Main Reading Room of the New York Public Library, a block from Grand Central, is open to all and remains the city's preeminent seat of learning, resting atop millions of available reference books.

Since 1970, New York has hosted an annual marathon. Originally run entirely within Manhattan's Central Park, the race course now begins on Staten Island, crosses the Verrazano Narrows Bridge, goes through the remaining four boroughs, and ends on the west side of Central Park. The marathon attracts over 20,000 contestants from around the world, and an estimated two million spectators. On race day, thousands of cheerful volunteers hand out much-needed items to the runners, including 200,000 bottles of water, 22,000 gallons of Gatorade, and 40,000 adhesive bandages.

There is nothing more poetic and terrible than the skyscrapers' battle with the heavens that cover them. Snow, rain, and mist highlight, drench, or conceal the vast towers, but those towers, hostile to mystery and blind to any sort of play, shear off the rain's tresses and shine their three thousand swords through the soft swan of the fog.

— Federico Garcia Lorca, *"A Poet in New York"*

I get so sentimental when I see

How perfect perfection can be. . . .

— Fred Astaire, *Top Hat*

A familiar site, but usually in white, the Chrysler Building's art deco top hat is lit temporarily in red in connection with a tourism promotion to "paint the town red."

FOLLOWING PAGE RIGHT: Brooklyn Bridge was the first steel cable suspension bridge in the world and was later joined in crossing the East River by the Williamsburg Bridge, Manhattan Bridge, and Queensboro Bridge.

Blue mountainous clouds
at the end of the street, a coppery
sheen below that,
below that straight brown lines, gray,
a shifting white bit in the corner
where the bay
slaps itself. Late sun drains
one side of Manhattan, slips off
to distant parts
as revelers and late risers walk off
their divisions, come together
with themselves.
Tourists jostle
like fitful birds settling for the
night.
Brooklyn waterfront, Governors Island
are crusted with mechanical devices,
docks,
and cranes with their arms folded back.
Dusk brings its colorful peace to
the lower
parts of the island, settles small
disputes of daylight
around the fish market, leans hard
against certain buildings
and retires. . . .

— Charlie Smith, *from "Poems Without Words"*

One of Brooklyn's many elegant, turn-of-the-century brownstone
schoolhouses is warmed by a late afternoon sun.

Conceived when Brooklyn was still an independent city, the Brooklyn Museum, near the borough's Prospect Park and Botanic Garden, was intended to be four times larger than its present size. It houses one of the world's great collections of Egyptian art (rivaling the Met's collection) and important examples of the Hudson River School of painting.

RIGHT: The Byzantine-Romanesque tower of the Williamsburgh Savings Bank, completed in 1929, rises above the façade of the neighboring Brooklyn Academy of Music, completed in 1908.

ABOVE: An architectural detail from the Brooklyn Academy of Music.

In a perfect world, *we'd all be Yankees.*
— Rick Horowitz

Home to the Bronx Bombers (a.k.a. New York Yankees), the House that Ruth Built (a.k.a. Yankees Stadium) is located in the Bronx, where related cuisine, outdoor art, and (lately) World Series celebrations abound.

FOLLOWING PAGES: Named for Giovanni da Verrazano, the first European to see (later named) New York Harbor, the Verrazano Narrows Bridge connects residents of Staten Island with Brooklyn and the rest of New York City.

LEFT: The Victorian-era, glass Conservatory, modeled after the Palm Conservatory of the Royal Botanical Gardens in England, is the focal point of the New York Botanical Garden, located near the Bronx Zoo.

ABOVE: The Bronx Zoo/Wildlife Conservation Park opened in 1899 and was the first zoo to employ a full-time veterinarian (1902) and to open an animal hospital (1916).

And New York is *the most beautiful city*
in the world? It is not far from it. No urban night is like the
night there. . . . Squares after squares of flame, set up
and cut into the ether. Here is our poetry,
for we have pulled down the stars to our will.

— Ezra Pound

RIGHT: Downtown Manhattan and the World Financial Center are seen from across the East River.

FOLLOWING PAGE LEFT: Each Christmas since 1952, a twelve-story cross of lights has adorned the Helmsley Building, which sits astride Park Avenue, just north of the Pan Am (now Metlife) Building and Grand Central Terminal.

FOLLOWING PAGE RIGHT: One mile north of the Battery and wedged into an imperfect triangular park is Manhattan's City Hall, built in 1811 of white marble (and temporarily adorned here with bunting for a Yankees World Series victory parade).

"A hundred times have I thought
New York is a catastrophe and 50 times:
it is a beautiful catastrophe."

— **Le Corbusier**

And round the corner was the more august precinct of the Fifth Avenue, taking its origin at this point with a spacious and confident air which already marked it for high destinies. I know not whether it is owing to the tenderness of early associations, but this portion of New York appears to many persons the most delectable. It has a kind of established repose which is not of frequent occurrence in other quarters of the long, shrill city; it has a riper, richer, more honourable look than any of the upper ramifications of the great longitudinal thoroughfare— the look of having had something of a social history.

— **Henry James,** *Washington Square*

LEFT: The Washington Square Arch, commemorating the hundredth anniversary of Washington's oath of office, marks the beginning of Fifth Avenue.

ABOVE: On warm weather weekends, Washington Square, in the heart of Greenwich Village, is often brimming with street performers.

ABOVE: The ConEd Tower (short for Consolidated Edison, the city's power company), looks with disdain upon its newer Union Square neighbor, the Zechendorf apartment towers.

TOP RIGHT: An architectural detail from the old General Electric building located on Lexington Avenue in Midtown.

BOTTOM RIGHT: The Time Café, located in the East Village on Lafayette, has withstood test of its namesake in the winnowing business of restaurateurs.

FOLLOWING PAGES: Since 1974, a stretch of Sixth Avenue through Greenwich Village has been the site of an annual come-one-come-all Halloween Parade.

The Staten Island Ferry churns a golden New York Harbor as it prepares to pass the Statue of Liberty.

Not like the brazen giant of Greek fame,

With conquering limbs astride from land to land;

Here at our sea-washed, sunset gates shall stand

A mighty woman with a torch, whose flame

is the imprisoned lightning, and her name

Mother of Exiles. From her beacon-hand

Glows the world-wide welcome; her mild eyes command

The air-bridged harbor that twin cities frame.

"Keep ancient lands, your storied pomp!" cries she

With silent lips. "Give me your tired, your poor,

Your huddled masses yearning to breathe free,

The wretched refuse of your teeming shore.

Send these, the homeless, tempest-lost to me,

I lift my lamp beside the golden door!"

— Emma Lazarus, *"The New Colossus"*

ABOVE: Putting the "dow" in downtown is Manhattan's Financial District. Its tangle of streets and alleyways preceded the more easily navigated grid of streets and avenues that by 1811 began to take shape to the north of the district.

RIGHT: The graveyard of Trinity Church, located at the start of Wall Street, is home to some of the city's most famous permanent residents, including signers of the Declaration of Independence (Francis Lewis) and of the U.S. Constitution (Hugh Williamson).

FOLLOWING PAGE RIGHT: Flags such as these are a familiar sight on many Fifth Avenue façades.

FOLLOWING PAGE LEFT: New York has had an active securities market since Alexander Hamilton, as Secretary of the Treasury, issued bonds to repay debts of the American Revolution.

LEFT: The copper-topped Woolworth Building rising against the backdrop of the lines of the World Trade Center, was once—like a good many other New York buildings—the tallest building in the world. Indeed, President Woodrow Wilson had the honor, from a specially rigged switch at the White House, of turning on all at once the building's electrified lights. Beside it is the top of Manhattan Boro Hall.

ABOVE: A watered-down view of the World Trade Center.

FOLLOWING PAGES: Chinatown faithfully continues to keep intact the many religious and cultural customs of old China, including its annual New Year's Parade, albeit with the recorded sounds of (outlawed) firecrackers.

ABOVE: Chefs at the Jean Georges restaurant, located at One Central Park West, confer during their nightly rounds of four-star preparations.

LEFT: New York Noodletown, located on the Bowery in Chinatown, hangs its roasted meats in the window to tempt passersby.

New York's Lower East Side remains a melting pot of the broadest variety where
shoppers can find great bargains on anything from pickles to platform shoes.

Bloomingdale's, as seen from across Lexington Avenue, bids a warm
welcome to holiday shoppers and passersby.

A splendid desert—a domed and steepled solitude,
where the stranger is lonely in the
midst of a million of his race.

— Mark Twain

The base of this brightly painted newsstand at the intersection of Bowery and Canal serves to remind its readers of the origin of the word "news."

ABOVE: This Midtowner puts a new spin on turning blue from the cold.

RIGHT: The old police station, on Lafayette Street in SoHo, could suffice for many a state's capitol building.

Every Wednesday and Saturday, area farmers and food purveyors
sell their fresh produce to patrons of the open-air farmer's market
of Union Square.

ABOVE: Delmonico's, a Financial District landmark, was once the best known restaurant in the United States. Among the many familiar dishes that originated here are Baked Alaska and Lobster Newberg.

RIGHT: On West 23rd Street, Chelsea's principal cross-town thoroughfare, stands the Chelsea Hotel. In operation since 1884, its notable guests include Mark Twain (see page 140), O. Henry (p. 84), Thomas Wolfe, Dylan Thomas, and Arthur Miller.

FOLLOWING PAGES: SoHo's many bistros, such as this one, offer a welcome respite from the siren's call of the fashionable neighborhood's boutiques and galleries.

New York was practical and insane. . . . It decided to grow along a grid, ignoring bumps, ditches, and heights, and the particular bend of its rivers. It would be a phantom grid of 2028 blocks, where anything that was built upon them could be removed at will. So we have the Empire State Building dug into the old cradle of the Waldorf-Astoria. And the Waldorf is shoved onto another grid. We have a Madison Square Garden on Madison Square and then the Garden starts to float, like a gondola on the grid. It reappears uptown, caters to circuses and rodeos, the Rangers and the Knicks, becomes a parking lot, and the Garden is born again over the new Penn Station. It's an ugly glass tank, but who cares? Nothing is sacred except the grid. And the grid doesn't allow for memory and remorse.

—**Jerome Charyn,** *Metropolis*

ABOVE: Offering a Cubist's view of midtown Manhattan, the Javits Center, located along a five-block parcel fronting Eleventh Avenue, is New York's principal convention space.

RIGHT, *TOP:* The mansard roof and arched windows of the Pierre Hotel (its top floor is a private residence) stand out against the white marble and black glass curtain of the GM Building. *MIDDLE:* A closeup of one of two 330-foot spires of St. Patrick's Cathedral. Now nestled within a modern Midtown, its original construction was halted for a several year period during and following the Civil War. *BOTTOM:* As much an obelisk of 1980s excess as it is a Fifth Avenue fixture, Trump Tower remains a favorite destination for many.

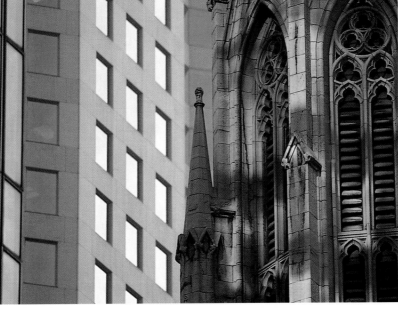

New York . . . is a city of geometric heights, a petrified desert of grids and lattices, an inferno of greenish abstraction under a flat sky, a real Metropolis from which man is absent by his very accumulation.

— **Roland Barthes**

RIGHT: The majestic, cascading façade of Rockefeller Center's RCA (now GE) Building. In the distance are the beginnings of the Hudson River Palisades.

PREVIOUS PAGE LEFT: Elegant terra-cotta cornices appoint each of the Flatiron's floors, floodlit (a rare occasion) while a film crew shoots a commercial nearby.

PREVIOUS PAGE RIGHT: Rising gracefully above the scissors-like intersection of Broadway and Fifth Avenue, the Flatiron Building was christened the Fuller Building when completed in 1902, but gradually became better known for its famous footprint.

LEFT: Brightening an otherwise rainy day, the Macy's Thanksgiving Day Parade has lifted dampened spirits continuously since 1929.

ABOVE: Santa and his helpers head down Central Park West toward Macy's, their temporary residence for the Holidays. (Until Christmas Eve, of course.)

PREVIOUS PAGE LEFT: Standing resolutely upon his 70-foot granite pedestal, Christopher Columbus has his back turned to one of the many passing floats of the annual Macy's Thanksgiving Day Parade.

PREVIOUS PAGE RIGHT: A pair of policemen visit during the Macy's Thanksgiving Day Parade.

ABOVE: Mulberry Street, the principal artery of Manhattan's Little Italy is decked out for the Christmas Holidays.

RIGHT: The Cathedral Church of St. John the Divine, on the Upper West Side near Columbia University, is the largest cathedral in the world. So big in fact, Lady Liberty could attend services without tipping her torch!

FOLLOWING PAGE RIGHT: Pedestrians pass by the southwest corner of St. Patrick's Cathedral, located on Fifth Avenue.

FOLLOWING PAGE LEFT: St. John's remains under construction (as it has for over a hundred years) as stonecutters and their apprentices carve by hand the church's resplendent gothic detail.

had a friend who could not sleep, and he knew a few other people who had the same trouble, and we would watch the sky lighten and have a last drink with no ice and then go home in the early morning light, when the streets were clean and wet (had it rained in the night? we never knew) and the few cruising taxis still had their headlights on and the only color was the read and green of traffic signals.

— **Joan Didion,** *Goodbye to All That*

RIGHT: Cars cross the Triboro Bridge, one of Manhattan's principal connections to Long Island. For visitors en route to nearby LaGuardia Airport, the view from the bridge's main span offers one last skyline view of Manhattan.

PREVIOUS PAGES: Topped by a mooring mast for dirigibles, the Empire State Building was to serve (and did serve on one occasion) as Manhattan's midtown airport.

Credits